P9-DGN-845

· STICKEEN ·

John Muir

Illustrations by Carl Dennis Buell
Afterword by Malcolm Margolin

HEYDAY BOOKS, BERKELEY
IN CONJUNCTION WITH RICK HEIDE

Illustrations copyright © 1990 by Carl Dennis Buell
Afterword copyright © 1981 by Heyday Books
Text reprinted from the Houghton Mifflin edition of 1909.

ISBN: 0-930588-48-7
Library of Congress Catalog Card Number: 90-84443

Design by Sarah Levin
Typography by Archetype, Berkeley, CA

Printed in the United States of America
10 9 8 7 6 5 4 3 2 1

Published by Heyday Books
P.O. Box 9145 Berkeley, CA 94709

Stickeen

Contents

Stickeen · 1 ·

Afterword · 73 ·

Chronology of Muir's Life · 82 ·

· To Helen Muir ·
Lover of wildness
this icy storm-story
is affectionately
dedicated

IN THE SUMMER OF 1880 I set out from Fort Wrangel in a canoe to continue the exploration of the icy region of southeastern Alaska, begun in the fall of 1879. After the necessary provisions, blankets, etc., had been collected and stowed away, and my Indian crew were in their places ready to start, while a crowd of their relatives and friends on the wharf were bidding them good-by and good-luck, my companion, the Rev. S. H. Young, for whom we were waiting, at last came aboard, followed by a little black dog,

that immediately made himself at home
by curling up in a hollow among the
baggage. I like dogs, but this one seemed
so small and worthless that I objected to
his going, and asked the missionary why
he was taking him.

"Such a little helpless creature will
only be in the way," I said; "you had
better pass him up to the Indian boys
on the wharf, to be taken home to play
with the children. This trip is not likely
to be good for toy-dogs. The poor silly
thing will be in rain and snow for weeks
or months, and will require care like a
baby."

But his master assured me that he
would be no trouble at all; that he was
a perfect wonder of a dog, could endure

cold and hunger like a bear, swim like a seal, and was wondrous wise and cunning, etc., making out a list of virtues to show he might be the most interesting member of the party.

Nobody could hope to unravel the lines of his ancestry. In all the wonderfully mixed and varied dog-tribe I never saw any creature very much like him, though in some of his sly, soft, gliding motions and gestures he brought the fox to mind. He was short-legged and bunchy-bodied, and his hair, though smooth, was long and silky and slightly waved, so that when the wind was at his back it ruffled, making him look shaggy. At first sight his only noticeable feature was his fine tail, which was about as airy and shady

as a squirrel's, and was carried curling
forward almost to his nose. On closer
inspection you might notice his thin sen-
sitive ears, and sharp eyes with cunning
tan-spots above them. Mr. Young told
me that when the little fellow was a pup
about the size of a woodrat he was presented to his wife by an Irish prospector
at Sitka, and that on his arrival at Fort
Wrangel he was adopted with enthusiasm
by the Stickeen Indians as a sort of new
good-luck totem, was named "Stickeen"
for the tribe, and became a universal
favorite; petted, protected, and admired
wherever he went, and regarded as a
mysterious fountain of wisdom.

On our trip he soon proved himself a
queer character — odd, concealed, inde-

pendent, keeping invincibly quiet, and
doing many little puzzling things that
piqued my curiosity. As we sailed week
after week through the long intricate
channels and inlets among the innumerable islands and mountains of the coast,
he spent most of the dull days in sluggish
ease, motionless, and apparently as un-
observing as if in deep sleep. But I discovered that somehow he always knew
what was going on. When the Indians
were about to shoot at ducks or seals,
or when anything along the shore was
exciting our attention, he would rest his
chin on the edge of the canoe and calmly
look out like a dreamy-eyed tourist. And
when he heard us talking about making
a landing, he immediately roused himself

to see what sort of a place we were coming to, and made ready to jump overboard and swim ashore as soon as the canoe neared the beach. Then, with a vigorous shake to get rid of the brine in his hair, he ran into the woods to hunt small game. But though always the first out of the canoe, he was always the last to get into it. When we were ready to start he could never be found, and refused to come to our call. We soon found out, however, that though we could not see him at such times, he saw us, and from the cover of the briers and huckleberry bushes in the fringe of the woods was watching the canoe with wary eye. For as soon as we were fairly off he came trotting down the beach, plunged into the surf, and swam after us, knowing well that we would cease rowing and take him in. When the contrary little vagabond came alongside, he was lifted by the neck, held at arm's length a moment to drip, and dropped aboard. We tried to cure him of this trick by compelling him to swim a long way, as if we had a mind to abandon him; but this did no good: the longer the swim the better he seemed to like it.

Though capable of great idleness, he never failed to be ready for all sorts of adventures and excursions. One pitch-dark rainy night we landed about ten o'clock at the mouth of a salmon stream when the water was phosphorescent. The salmon were running, and the

myriad fins of the onrushing multitude were churning all the stream into a silvery glow, wonderfully beautiful and impressive in the ebon darkness. To get a good view of the show I set out with one of the Indians and sailed up through the midst of it to the foot of a rapid about half a mile from camp, where the swift current dashing over rocks made the luminous glow most glorious. Happening to look back down the stream, while the Indian was catching a few of the struggling fish, I saw a long spreading fan of light like the tail of a comet, which we thought must be made by some big strange animal that was pursuing us. On it came with its magnificent train, until we imagined we could see the monster's head and eyes; but it was only Stickeen, who, finding I had left the camp, came swimming after me to see what was up. When we camped early, the best hunter of the crew usually went to the woods for a deer, and Stickeen was sure to be at his heels, provided I had not gone out. For, strange to say, though I never carried a gun, he always followed me, forsaking the hunter and even his master to share my wanderings. The days that were too stormy for sailing I spent in the woods, or on the adjacent mountains, wherever my studies called me; and Stickeen always insisted on going with me, however wild the weather, gliding like a fox through dripping huckleberry bushes and thorny tangles of panax and rubus, scarce stirring their rain-laden leaves; wading and wallowing through snow, swimming icy streams, skipping over logs and rocks and the crevasses of glaciers with the patience and endurance of a determined mountaineer, never tiring or getting discouraged. Once he followed me over a glacier the surface of which was so crusty and rough that it cut his feet until every step was marked with blood; but he trotted on with Indian fortitude until I noticed his red track, and, taking pity on him, made him a set of moccasins out of a handkerchief. However great his troubles he never asked help or made any complaint, as if, like a philosopher, he had learned that without hard work and suffering there could be no pleasure worth having.

JOHN MUIR

Yet none of us was able to make out what Stickeen was really good for. He seemed to meet danger and hardships without anything like reason, insisted on having his own way, never obeyed an order, and the hunter could never set him on anything, or make him fetch the birds he shot. His equanimity was so steady it seemed due to want of feeling; ordinary storms were pleasures to him, and as for mere rain, he flourished in it like a vegetable. No matter what advances you might make, scarce a glance or a tail-wag would you get for your pains. But though he was apparently as cold as a glacier and about as impervious to fun, I tried hard to make his acquaintance, guessing there must be something worth while hidden beneath so much

· 13 ·

courage, endurance, and love of wild-weathery adventure. No superannuated mastiff or bulldog grown old in office surpassed this fluffy midget in stoic dignity. He sometimes reminded me of a small, squat, unshakable desert cactus. For he never displayed a single trace of the merry, tricksy, elfish fun of the terriers and collies that we all know, nor of their touching affection and devotion. Like children, most small dogs beg to be loved and allowed to love; but Stickeen seemed a very Diogenes, asking only to be let alone: a true child of the wilderness, holding the even tenor of his hidden life with the silence and serenity of nature. His strength of character lay in his eyes. They looked as old as the hills, and as

young, and as wild. I never tired of looking into them: it was like looking into a
landscape; but they were small and
rather deep-set, and had no explaining
lines around them to give out particulars.
I was accustomed to look into the faces
of plants and animals, and I watched the
little sphinx more and more keenly as
an interesting study. But there is no estimating the wit and wisdom concealed
and latent in our lower fellow mortals
until made manifest by profound experi-
ences; for it is through suffering that
dogs as well as saints are developed and
made perfect.

After we had explored the Sundum
and Takhoo fiords and their glaciers, we
sailed through Stephen's Passage into

Lynn Canal and thence through Icy Strait into Cross Sound, searching for unexplored inlets leading toward the great fountain ice-fields of the Fairweather Range. Here, while the tide was in our favor, we were accompanied by a fleet of icebergs drifting out to the ocean from Glacier Bay. Slowly we paddled around Vancouver's Point, Wimbleton, our frail canoe tossed like a feather on the massive heaving swells coming in past Cape Spenser. For miles the sound is bounded by precipitous mural cliffs, which, lashed with wave-spray and their heads hidden in clouds, looked terribly threatening and stern. Had our canoe been crushed or upset we could have made no landing here, for the cliffs, as high as those of

· 17 ·

Yosemite, sink sheer into deep water. Eagerly we scanned the wall on the north side for the first sign of an opening fiord or harbor, all of us anxious except Stickeen, who dozed in peace or gazed dreamily at the tremendous precipices when he heard us talking about them. At length we made the joyful discovery of the mouth of the inlet now called "Taylor Bay," and about five o'clock reached the head of it and encamped in a spruce grove near the front of a large glacier.

While camp was being made, Joe the hunter climbed the mountain wall on the east side of the fiord in pursuit of wild goats, while Mr. Young and I went to the glacier. We found that it is separated from the waters of the inlet by a tide-washed moraine, and extends, an abrupt barrier, all the way across from wall to wall of the inlet, a distance of about three miles. But our most interesting discovery was that it had recently advanced, though again slightly receding. A portion of the terminal moraine had been plowed up and shoved forward, uprooting and overwhelming the woods on the east side. Many of the trees were down and buried, or nearly so, others were leaning away from the ice-cliffs, ready to fall, and some stood erect, with the bottom of the ice-plow still beneath their roots and its lofty crystal spires towering high above their tops. The spectacle presented by these century-old trees standing close beside a spiry wall of ice, with their branches almost touching it, was most novel and striking. And when I climbed around the front, and a little way up the west side of the glacier, I found that it had swelled and increased in height and width in accordance with its advance, and carried away the outer ranks of trees on its bank.

On our way back to camp after these first observations I planned a far-and-wide excursion for the morrow. I awoke early, called not only by the glacier, which had been on my mind all night, but by a grand flood-storm. The wind was blowing a gale from the north and the rain was flying with the clouds in a wide passionate horizontal flood, as if it were all passing over the country instead of falling on it. The main perennial streams were booming high above their banks, and hundreds of new ones, roaring like the sea, almost covered the lofty gray walls of the inlet with white cascades and falls. I had intended making a cup of coffee and getting something like a breakfast before starting, but when I heard the storm and looked out I made haste to join it; for many of Nature's finest lessons are to be found in her storms, and if careful to keep in right relations with them, we may go safely abroad with them, rejoicing in the grandeur and beauty of their works and ways, and chanting with the old Norsemen, "The blast of the tempest aids our oars, the hurricane is our servant and drives us whither we wish to go." So, omitting breakfast, I put a piece of bread in my pocket and hurried away.

Mr. Young and the Indians were asleep, and so, I hoped, was Stickeen; but I had not gone a dozen rods before he left his bed in the tent and came boring through the blast after me. That a man should welcome storms for their exhilarating music and motion, and go forth to see God making landscapes, is reasonable enough; but what fascination could there be in such tremendous weather for a dog? Surely nothing akin to human enthusiasm for scenery or geology. Anyhow, on he came, breakfastless, through the choking blast. I stopped and did my best to turn him back. "Now don't," I said, shouting to make myself heard in the storm, "now don't, Stickeen. What has got into your queer noddle now? You must be daft. This wild day has nothing for you. There is no game abroad, nothing but weather. Go back to camp and keep warm, get a good breakfast with your master, and be sensible for once. I can't carry you all day or feed you, and this storm will kill you."

But Nature, it seems, was at the bottom of the affair, and she gains her ends with dogs as well as with men, making us do as she likes, shoving and pulling us along her ways, however rough, all but killing us at times in getting her lessons driven hard home. After I had stopped again and again, shouting good warning advice, I saw that he was not to be shaken off; as well might the earth try to shake off the moon. I had once led his master into trouble, when he fell on one of the topmost jags of a mountain and dislocated his arm; now the turn of his humble companion was coming. The pitiful little wanderer just stood there in the wind, drenched and blinking, saying doggedly, "Where thou goest I will go." So at last I told him to come on if he must, and gave him a piece of the bread I had in my pocket; then we struggled on together, and thus began the most memorable of all my wild days.

The level flood, driving hard in our faces, thrashed and washed us wildly until we got into the shelter of a grove on the east side of the glacier near the front, where we stopped awhile for breath and to listen and look out. The exploration of the glacier was my main object, but the wind was too high to allow excursions over its open surface, where one might be dangerously shoved while balancing for a jump on the brink of a crevasse. In the mean time the storm was a fine study. Here the end of the glacier, descending an abrupt swell of resisting rock about five hundred feet high, leans forward and falls in ice cascades. And as the storm came down the glacier from the North, Stickeen and I were beneath the main current of the blast, while favorably located to see and

hear it. What a psalm the storm was singing, and how fresh the smell of the washed earth and leaves, and how sweet the still small voices of the storm! Detached wafts and swirls were coming through the woods, with music from the leaves and branches and furrowed boles, and even from the splintered rocks and ice-crags overhead, many of the tones soft and low and flute-like, as if each leaf and tree, crag and spire were a tuned reed. A broad torrent, draining the side of the glacier, now swollen by scores of new streams from the mountains, was rolling boulders along its rocky channel, with thudding, bumping, muffled sounds, rushing towards the bay with tremendous energy, as if in haste to get out of the mountains; the waters above and be-neath calling to each other, and all to the ocean, their home.

Looking southward from our shelter, we had this great torrent and the forested mountain wall above it on our left, the spiry ice-crags on our right, and smooth gray gloom ahead. I tried to draw the marvelous scene in my note-book, but the rain blurred the page in spite of all my pains to shelter it, and the sketch was almost worthless. When the wind began to abate, I traced the east side of the glacier. All the trees standing on the edge of the woods were barked and bruised, showing high-ice mark in a very telling way, while tens of thousands of those that had stood for centuries on the bank of the glacier farther out lay crushed and being crushed. In many places I could see down fifty feet or so beneath the margin of the glacier-mill, where trunks from one to two feet in diameter were being ground to pulp against outstanding rock-ribs and bosses of the bank.

About three miles above the front of the glacier I climbed to the surface of it by means of axe-steps made easy for Stickeen. As far as the eye could reach, the level, or nearly level, glacier stretched away indefinitely beneath the gray sky, a seemingly boundless prairie of ice. The rain continued, and grew colder, which I did not mind, but a dim snowy look in the drooping clouds made me hesitate about

venturing far from land. No trace of the
west shore was visible, and in case the
clouds should settle and give snow, or
the wind again become violent, I feared
getting caught in a tangle of crevasses.
Snow-crystals, the flowers of the mountain clouds, are frail, beautiful things,
but terrible when flying on storm-winds
in darkening, benumbing swarms, or,
when welded together into glaciers
full of deadly crevasses. Watching the
weather, I sauntered about on the crystal
sea. For a mile or two out I found the
ice remarkably safe. The marginal crevasses were mostly narrow, while the few
wider ones were easily avoided by passing around them, and the clouds began
to open here and there.

Thus encouraged, I at last pushed out for the other side; for Nature can make us do anything she likes. At first we made rapid progress, and the sky was not very threatening, while I took bearings occasionally with a pocket compass to enable me to find my way back more surely in case the storm should become blinding; but the structure lines of the glacier were my main guide. Toward the west side we came to a closely crevassed section in which we had to make long, narrow tacks and doublings, tracing the edges of tremendous transverse and longitudinal crevasses, many of which were from twenty to thirty feet wide, and perhaps a thousand feet deep — beautiful and awful. In working a way through them

I was severely cautious, but Stickeen came on as unhesitating as the flying clouds. The widest crevasse that I could jump he would leap without so much as halting to take a look at it. The weather was now making quick changes, scattering bits of dazzling brightness through the wintry gloom; at rare intervals, when the sun broke forth wholly free, the glacier was seen from shore to shore with a bright array of encompassing mountains partly revealed, wearing the clouds as garments, while the prairie bloomed and sparkled with irised light from myriads of washed crystals. Then suddenly all the glorious show would be darkened and blotted out.

Stickeen seemed to care for none of

these things, bright or dark, nor for the crevasses, wells, moulins, or swift flashing streams into which he might fall. The little adventurer was only about two years old, yet nothing seemed novel to him, nothing daunted him. He showed neither caution nor curiosity, wonder nor fear, but bravely trotted on as if glaciers were playgrounds. His stout, muffled body seemed all one skipping muscle, and it was truly wonderful to see how swiftly and to all appearance heedlessly he flashed across nerve-trying chasms six or eight feet wide. His courage was so unwavering that it seemed to be due to dullness of perception, as if he were only blindly bold; and I kept warning him to be careful. For we had been close

companions on so many wilderness trips
that I had formed the habit of talking to
him as if he were a boy and understood
every word.

We gained the west shore in about
three hours; the width of the glacier here
being about seven miles. Then I pushed
northward in order to see as far back as
possible into the fountains of the Fairweather Mountains, in case the clouds
should rise. The walking was easy along
the margin of the forest, which, of
course, like that on the other side, had
been invaded and crushed by the swollen,
overflowing glacier. In an hour or so,
after passing a massive headland, we
came suddenly on a branch of the glacier, which, in the form of a magnificent

ice-cascade two miles wide, was pouring over the rim of the main basin in a
westerly direction, its surface broken
into wave-shaped blades and shattered
blocks, suggesting the wildest updash-
ing, heaving, plunging motion of a great
river cataract. Tracing it down three or
four miles, I found that it discharged into
a lake, filling it with icebergs.

I would gladly have followed the lake
outlet to tide-water, but the day was already far spent, and the threatening sky
called for haste on the return trip to get
off the ice before dark. I decided therefore to go no farther, and, after taking
a general view of the wonderful region,
turned back, hoping to see it again under
more favorable auspices. We made good

speed up the cañon of the great ice-
torrent, and out on the main glacier until
we had left the west shore about two
miles behind us. Here we got into a difficult network of crevasses, the gathering
clouds began to drop misty fringes, and
soon the dreaded snow came flying thick
and fast. I now began to feel anxious
about finding a way in the blurring
storm. Stickeen showed no trace of fear.
He was still the same silent, able little
hero. I noticed, however, that after the
storm-darkness came on he kept close
up behind me. The snow urged us to
make still greater haste, but at the same
time hid our way. I pushed on as best I
could, jumping innumerable crevasses,
and for every hundred rods or so of direct

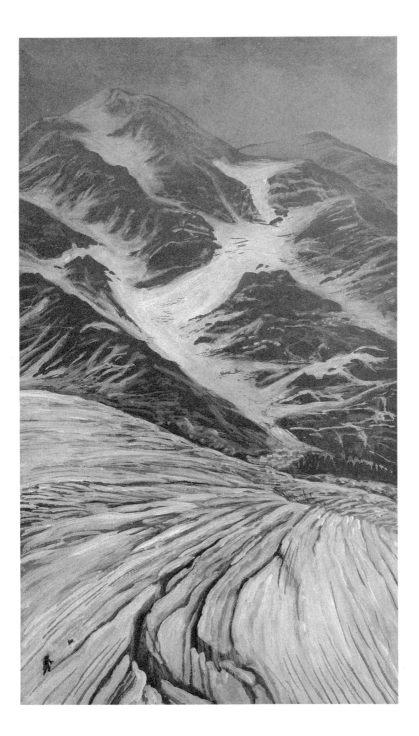

advance traveling a mile in doubling up
and down in the turmoil of chasms and
dislocated ice-blocks. After an hour or
two of this work we came to a series of
longitudinal crevasses of appalling
width, and almost straight and regular
in trend, like immense furrows. These I
traced with firm nerve, excited and
strengthened by the danger, making
wide jumps, poising cautiously on their
dizzy edges after cutting hollows for my
feet before making the spring, to avoid
possible slipping or any uncertainty on
the farther sides, where only one trial is
granted — exercise at once frightful and
inspiring. Stickeen followed seemingly
without effort.

Many a mile we thus traveled, mostly

up and down, making but little real head-
way in crossing, running instead of walking most of the time as the danger of
being compelled to spend the night on
the glacier became threatening. Stickeen
seemed able for anything. Doubtless we
could have weathered the storm for one
night, dancing on a flat spot to keep from
freezing, and I faced the threat without
feeling anything like despair; but we
were hungry and wet, and the wind from
the mountains was still thick with snow
and bitterly cold, so of course that night
would have seemed a very long one. I
could not see far enough through the
blurring snow to judge in which general
direction the least dangerous route lay,
while the few dim, momentary glimpses

STICKEEN

I caught of mountains through rifts in the flying clouds were far from encouraging either as weather signs or as guides. I had simply to grope my way from crevasse to crevasse, holding a general direction by the ice-structure, which was not to be seen everywhere, and partly by the wind. Again and again I was put to my mettle, but Stickeen followed easily, his nerve apparently growing more unflinching as the danger increased. So it always is with mountaineers when hard beset. Running hard and jumping, holding every minute of the remaining daylight, poor as it was, precious, we doggedly persevered and tried to hope that every difficult crevasse we overcame would prove to be the last of its kind.

But on the contrary, as we advanced they became more deadly trying.

At length our way was barred by a very wide and straight crevasse, which I traced rapidly northward a mile or so without finding a crossing or hope of one; then down the glacier about as far, to where it united with another uncrossable crevasse. In all this distance of perhaps two miles there was only one place where I could possibly jump it, but the width of this jump was the utmost I dared attempt, while the danger of slipping on the farther side was so great that I was loath to try it. Furthermore, the side I was on was about a foot higher than the other, and even with this advantage the crevasse seemed dangerously wide. One is liable to underestimate the width of crevasses where the magnitudes in general are great. I therefore stared at this one mighty keenly, estimating its width and the shape of the edge on the farther side, until I thought that I could jump it if necessary, but that in case I should be compelled to jump back from the lower side I might fail. Now, a cautious mountaineer seldom takes a step on unknown ground which seems at all dangerous that he cannot retrace in case he should be stopped by unseen obstacles ahead. This is the rule of mountaineers who live long, and, though in haste, I compelled myself to sit down and calmly deliberate before I broke it.

Retracing my devious path in imagination as if it were drawn on a chart, I saw that I was recrossing the glacier a mile or two farther up stream than the course pursued in the morning, and that I was now entangled in a section I had not before seen. Should I risk this dangerous jump, or try to regain the woods on the west shore, make a fire, and have only hunger to endure while waiting for a new day? I had already crossed so broad a stretch of dangerous ice that I saw it would be difficult to get back to the woods through the storm, before dark, and the attempt would most likely result in a dismal nightdance on the glacier; while just beyond the present barrier the surface seemed more promising, and the east shore was now perhaps about as near as the west. I was therefore eager to go on. But this wide jump was a dreadful obstacle.

At length, because of the dangers already behind me, I determined to venture against those that might be ahead, jumped and landed well, but with so little to spare that I more than ever dreaded being compelled to take that jump back from the lower side. Stickeen followed, making nothing of it, and we ran eagerly forward, hoping we were leaving all our troubles behind. But within the distance of a few hundred yards we were stopped by the widest crevasse yet encountered. Of course I made haste to explore it, hoping all might yet be remedied by finding a bridge or a way around either

end. About three-fourths of a mile up-
stream I found that it united with the
one we had just crossed, as I feared it
would. Then, tracing it down, I found it
joined the same crevasse at the lower
end also, maintaining throughout its
whole course a width of forty to fifty
feet. Thus to my dismay I discovered
that we were on a narrow island about
two miles long, with two barely possible
ways of escape: one back by the way we
came, the other ahead by an almost inaccessible sliver-bridge that crossed the
great crevasse from near the middle of it!

After this nerve-trying discovery I ran
back to the sliver-bridge and cautiously
examined it. Crevasses, caused by strains
from variations in the rate of motion of

different parts of the glacier and con-
vexities in the channel, are mere cracks
when they first open, so narrow as hardly
to admit the blade of a pocket-knife, and
gradually widen according to the extent
of the strain and the depth of the glacier.
Now some of these cracks are inter-
rupted, like the cracks in wood, and in
opening, the strip of ice between overlap-
ping ends is dragged out, and may main-
tain a continuous connection between
the sides, just as the two sides of a slivered
crack in wood that is being split are con-
nected. Some crevasses remain open for
months or even years, and by the melting
of their sides continue to increase in
width long after the opening strain has
ceased; while the sliver-bridges, level on

top at first and perfectly safe, are at length melted to thin, vertical, knife-edged blades, the upper portion being most exposed to the weather; and since the exposure is greatest in the middle, they at length curve downward like the cables of suspension bridges. This one was evidently very old, for it had been weathered and wasted until it was the most dangerous and inaccessible that ever lay in my way. The width of the crevasse was here about fifty feet, and the sliver crossing diagonally was about seventy feet long; its thin knife-edge near the middle was depressed twenty-five or thirty feet below the level of the glacier, and the upcurving ends were attached to the sides eight or ten feet below the brink. Getting down the nearly vertical wall to the end of the sliver and up the other side were the main difficulties, and they seemed all but insurmountable. Of the many perils encountered in my years of wandering on mountains and glaciers none seemed so plain and stern and merciless as this. And it was presented when we were wet to the skin and hungry, the sky dark with quick driving snow, and the night near. But we were forced to face it. It was a tremendous necessity.

Beginning, not immediately above the sunken end of the bridge, but a little to one side, I cut a deep hollow on the brink for my knees to rest in. Then, leaning over, with my short-handled axe I cut a step sixteen or eighteen inches below, which on account of the sheerness of the wall was necessarily shallow. That step, however, was well made; its floor sloped slightly inward and formed a good hold for my heels. Then, slipping cautiously upon it, and crouching as low as possible, with my left side toward the wall, I steadied myself against the wind with my left hand in a slight notch, while with the right I cut other similar steps and notches in succession, guarding against losing balance by glinting of the axe, or by wind-gusts, for life and death were in every stroke and in the niceness of finish of every foothold.

After the end of the bridge was reached I chipped it down until I had made a level platform six or eight inches wide, and it was a trying thing to poise on this little slippery platform while bending over to get safely astride of the sliver. Crossing was then comparatively easy by chipping off the sharp edge with short, careful strokes, and hitching forward an inch or two at a time, keeping my balance with my knees pressed against the sides. The tremendous abyss on either hand I studiously ignored. To me the edge of that blue sliver was then all the world. But the most trying part of the adventure, after working my way across inch by inch and chipping another small platform, was to rise from the safe position astride and to cut a step-ladder in the nearly vertical face of the wall, — chipping, climbing, holding on with feet

and fingers in mere notches. At such times one's whole body is eye, and common skill and fortitude are replaced by power beyond our call or knowledge. Never before had I been so long under deadly strain. How I got up that cliff I could never tell. The thing seemed to have been done by somebody else. I never have held death in contempt, though in the course of my explorations I have oftentimes felt that to meet one's fate on a noble mountain, or in the heart of a glacier, would be blessed as compared with death from disease, or from some shabby lowland accident. But the best death, quick and crystal-pure, set so glaringly open before us, is hard enough to face, even though we feel gratefully sure that we have already had happiness enough for a dozen lives.

But poor Stickeen, the wee, hairy, sleekit beastie, think of him! When I had decided to dare the bridge, and while I was on my knees chipping a hollow on the rounded brow above it, he came behind me, pushed his head past my shoulder, looked down and across, scanned the sliver and its approaches with his mysterious eyes, then looked me in the face with a startled air of surprise and concern, and began to mutter and whine; saying as plainly as if speaking with words, "Surely, you are not going into that awful place." This was the first time I had seen him gaze deliberately into a crevasse, or into my face with an eager, speaking, troubled look. That he should have recognized and appreciated the danger at the first glance showed wonderful sagacity. Never before had the daring midget seemed to know that ice was slippery or that there was any such thing as danger anywhere. His looks and tones of voice when he began to complain and speak his fears were so human that I unconsciously talked to him in sympathy as I would to a frightened boy, and in trying to calm his fears perhaps in some measure moderated my own. "Hush your fears, my boy," I said, "we will get across safe, though it is not going to be easy. No right way is easy in this rough world. We must risk our lives to save them. At the worst we can only slip, and then how grand a grave we will have, and by and by our nice bones will do good in the terminal moraine."

But my sermon was far from reassuring him: he began to cry, and after taking another piercing look at the tremendous gulf, ran away in desperate excitement, seeking some other crossing. By the time he got back, baffled of course, I had made a step or two. I dared not look back, but he made himself heard; and when he saw that I was certainly bent on crossing he cried aloud in despair. The danger was enough to daunt anybody, but it seems wonderful that he should have been able to weigh and appreciate it so justly. No mountaineer could have seen it more quickly or judged it more wisely, discriminating between real and apparent peril.

When I gained the other side, he screamed louder than ever, and after running back and forth in vain search for a way of escape, he would return to the brink of the crevasse above the bridge, moaning and wailing as if in the bitterness of death. Could this be the silent, philosophic Stickeen? I shouted encouragement, telling him the bridge was not as bad as it looked, that I had left it flat and safe for his feet, and he could walk it easily. But he was afraid to try. Strange so small an animal should be capable of such big, wise fears. I called again and again in a reassuring tone to come on and fear nothing; that he could come if he would only try. He would hush for a moment, look down again at the bridge, and shout his un-shakable conviction that he could never, never come that way; then lie back in despair, as if howling, "O-o-oh! what a place! No-o-o, I can never go-o-o down there!" His natural composure and cour-age had vanished utterly in a tumultuous storm of fear. Had the danger been less, his distress would have seemed ridicu-lous. But in this dismal, merciless abyss lay the shadow of death, and his heart-rending cries might well have called Heaven to his help. Perhaps they did. So hidden before, he was now transpar-ent, and one could see the workings of his heart and mind like the movements of a clock out of its case. His voice and gestures, hopes and fears, were so perfectly human that none could mistake them; while he seemed to understand every word of mine. I was troubled at the thought of having to leave him out all night, and of the danger of not finding him in the morning. It seemed impossible to get him to venture. To compel him to try through fear of being abandoned, I started off as if leaving him to his fate, and disappeared back of a hummock; but this did no good; he only lay down and moaned in utter hopeless misery. So, after hiding a few minutes, I went back to the brink of the crevasse and in a severe tone of voice shouted across to him that now I must certainly leave him,

I could wait no longer, and that, if he would not come, all I could promise was that I would return to seek him next day. I warned him that if he went back to the woods the wolves would kill him, and finished by urging him once more by words and gestures to come on, come on.

He knew very well what I meant, and at last, with the courage of despair, hushed and breathless, he crouched down on the brink in the hollow I had made for my knees, pressed his body against the ice as if trying to get the advantage of the friction of every hair, gazed into the first step, put his little feet together and slid them slowly, slowly over the edge and down into it, bunching all four in it and almost standing on his

head. Then, without lifting his feet, as well as I could see through the snow, he slowly worked them over the edge of the step and down into the next and the next in succession in the same way, and gained the end of the bridge. Then, lifting his feet with the regularity and slowness of the vibrations of a seconds pendulum, as if counting and measuring *one-two-three*, holding himself steady against the gusty wind, and giving separate attention to each little step, he gained the foot of the cliff, while I was on my knees leaning over to give him a lift should he succeed in getting within reach of my arm. Here he halted in dead silence, and it was here I feared he might fail, for dogs are poor climbers. I had no cord.

If I had had one, I would have dropped a noose over his head and hauled him up. But while I was thinking whether an available cord might be made out of clothing, he was looking keenly into the series of notched steps and finger-holds I had made, as if counting them, and fixing the position of each one of them in his mind. Then suddenly up he came in a springy rush, hooking his paws into the steps and notches so quickly that I could not see how it was done, and whizzed past my head, safe at last!

And now came a scene! "Well done, well done, little boy! Brave boy!" I cried, trying to catch and caress him; but he would not be caught. Never before or since have I seen anything like so passionate a revulsion from the depths of despair to exultant, triumphant, uncontrollable joy. He flashed and darted hither and thither as if fairly demented, screaming and shouting, swirling round and round in giddy loops and circles like a leaf in a whirlwind, lying down, and rolling over and over, sidewise and heels over head, and pouring forth a tumultuous flood of hysterical cries and sobs and gasping mutterings. When I ran up to him to shake him, fearing he might die of joy, he flashed off two or three hundred yards, his feet in a mist of motion; then, turning suddenly, came back in a wild rush and launched himself at my face, almost knocking me down, all the time screeching and screaming and shouting as if saying, "Saved! saved! saved!" Then away again, dropping suddenly at times with his feet in the air, trembling and fairly sobbing. Such passionate emotion was enough to kill him. Moses' stately song of triumph after escaping the Egyptians and the Red Sea was nothing to it. Who could have guessed the capacity of the dull, enduring little fellow for all that most stirs this mortal frame? Nobody could have helped crying with him!

But there is nothing like work for toning down excessive fear or joy. So I ran ahead, calling him in as gruff a voice as I could command to come on and stop his nonsense, for we had far to go and it would soon be dark. Neither of us

feared another trial like this. Heaven would surely count one enough for a lifetime. The ice ahead was gashed by thousands of crevasses, but they were common ones. The joy of deliverance burned in us like fire, and we ran without fatigue, every muscle with immense rebound glorying in its strength. Stickeen flew across everything in his way, and not till dark did he settle into his normal fox-like trot. At last the cloudy mountains came in sight, and we soon felt the solid rock beneath our feet, and were safe. Then came weakness. Danger had vanished, and so had our strength. We tottered down the lateral moraine in the dark, over boulders and tree trunks, through the bushes and devil-club thickets

of the grove where we had sheltered our-
selves in the morning, and across the
level mud-slope of the terminal moraine.
We reached camp about ten o'clock, and
found a big fire and a big supper. A party
of Hoona Indians had visited Mr. Young,
bringing a gift of porpoise meat and wild
strawberries, and Hunter Joe had brought
in a wild goat. But we lay down, too
tired to eat much, and soon fell into a
troubled sleep. The man who said, "The
harder the toil, the sweeter the rest,"
never was profoundly tired. Stickeen
kept springing up and muttering in his
sleep, no doubt dreaming that he was
still on the brink of the crevasse; and so
did I, that night and many others long
afterward, when I was over-tired.

Thereafter Stickeen was a changed dog. During the rest of the trip, instead of holding aloof, he always lay by my side, tried to keep me constantly in sight, and would hardly accept a morsel of food, however tempting, from any hand but mine. At night, when all was quiet about the camp-fire, he would come to me and rest his head on my knee with a look of devotion as if I were his god. And often as he caught my eye he seemed to be trying to say, "Wasn't that an awful time we had together on the glacier?"

Nothing in after years has dimmed that Alaska storm-day. As I write it all comes rushing and roaring to mind as if I were again in the heart of it. Again I

see the gray flying clouds with their rain-
floods and snow, the ice-cliffs towering
above the shrinking forest, the majestic
ice-cascade, the vast glacier outspread
before its white mountain fountains, and
in the heart of it the tremendous crevasse, — emblem of the valley of the
shadow of death, — low clouds trailing
over it, the snow falling into it; and on
its brink I see little Stickeen, and I hear
his cries for help and his shouts of joy.
I have known many dogs, and many a
story I could tell of their wisdom and
devotion; but to none do I owe so much
as to Stickeen. At first the least promising and least known of my dog-friends,
he suddenly became the best known of
them all. Our storm-battle for life

brought him to light, and through him as through a window I have ever since been looking with deeper sympathy into all my fellow mortals.

None of Stickeen's friends knows what finally became of him. After my work for the season was done I departed for California, and I never saw the dear little fellow again. In reply to anxious inquiries his master wrote me that in the summer of 1883 he was stolen by a tourist at Fort Wrangel and taken away on a steamer. His fate is wrapped in mystery. Doubtless he has left this world — crossed the last crevasse — and gone to another. But he will not be forgotten. To me Stickeen is immortal.

Afterword

JOHN MUIR met the Reverend S. Hall Young for the first time in the summer of 1879, a year before the adventure with Stickeen. Young, a missionary among the Tlinget Indians, describes Muir among the passengers arriving at Fort Wrangell, Alaska: "Standing a little apart from them as the steamboat drew to the dock, his peering blue eyes already eagerly scanning the islands and mountains, was a lean, sinewy man of forty, with waving, reddish-brown hair and beard, and shoulders slightly stooped. He wore a Scotch cap and a long, gray tweed ulster, which I have always since associated with him."

A strong and immediate friendship grew up between John Muir and the Reverend Young, and shortly after their first meeting they took off together for a day of mountain climbing. To climb with Muir was an experience no one ever forgot. Young described it in his book, *Alaska Days With John Muir:* "There was never an instant when both feet and hands were not in play, and often elbows, knees, thighs, upper arms, and even chin must grip and hold. Clambering up a steep slope . . . pulling up smooth rock-faces by sheer strength of arm and chinning over the edge, leaping fissures, sliding flat around a dangerous rock-breast, testing crumbling spurs before risking his weight, always going up, up, no hesitation, no pause — that was Muir!"

Young struggled to keep pace. In years past he had repeatedly dislocated both arms, and as he pulled himself up he felt the strain on his sockets. But, eager to impress Muir and keep up with him, he said nothing. On the descent, however, Young slipped, and as he reached out to catch himself both arms came entirely out of their joints. His arms useless and paralyzed, he slid down the rubble slope toward a cliff and a thousand-foot drop to a glacier below. He stopped at the very rim, his legs reaching out into the void.

"Grab that rock, man, just by your right hand," yelled Muir.

"My arms are out," Young gurgled desperately.

There was a pause. Then Muir's voice rang out, cheery and full of confidence: "Hold fast; I'm going to get you out of this." Muir began whistling and singing snatches of Scottish songs, calling his encouragement to Young. Young hung on — he never knew how — making his body as flat and heavy as possible, afraid even to twitch a muscle, wink an eyelid, or take a deep breath. Muir could not descend directly to where Young lay, but had to go along the slope and work his way back along the cliff edge — his foothold a precarious two-inch shelf. Upon reaching Young he grabbed him firmly and started back along the narrow shelf. Muir would pull Young toward him, set him in place, move a few inches, and then pull Young toward him again. In one place, needing his arms as well as his legs for support, he caught Young's collar in his teeth and holding him as a "panther with her cub" he climbed straight up a rock wall ten or twelve feet.

"It was utterly impossible," said Young, "Yet he did it!" Throughout the long night Muir carried and led the crippled Young down the mountain to help.

STICKEEN

Young's arms were later pulled back into their
sockets and he recovered rapidly. Although he
never went climbing high peaks with Muir again,
their friendship deepened. In October and
November of that year they set off in an open
canoe with a native crew to explore the Alexander
Archipelago, a group of some eleven hundred
wooded islands — Young to proselytize the Indians
who had never before seen a missionary; Muir to
study living glaciers, to botanize, and of course
to exult in the beauties and mysteries of the world.
The trip was true exploration. Alaska was then a
frontier, purchased from Russia only a dozen years
before. Its coast was largely uncharted, its interior
almost entirely unknown. Alaska was a large blank
area on the maps of the world. In their open,
red-cedar canoe Young and Muir visited bays and
penetrated fjords for the first time on record. A
major discovery of the trip was Glacier Bay and
the immense ice-river that later came to be called
Muir Glacier. They also caught a tantalizing
glimpse of Taylor Bay and the Taylor Glacier before being beaten back by weather — a glimpse
that was to haunt Muir all the next winter.

Muir returned to the San Francisco Bay Area

in December, and the next April, when he was nearly forty-two years old, he married Louie Wanda Strentzel. A few months later he once again boarded a boat and arrived in Alaska.

"Where's your wife?" asked a surprised Reverend Young.

"Man," exclaimed Muir, "have you forgotten? Don't you know we lost a glacier last fall? . . . Get your canoe and crew and let us be off!"

Thus began the voyage immortalized by the presence of Stickeen.

One hates to comment directly on the story of *Stickeen*; it is so perfect and exultant a story that one fears any additional words would merely diminish it. But perhaps it would be useful to explain aspects of the story that might have been more obvious to a nineteenth century reader than to one of today.

First was Muir's fascination with glaciers. In the ten years before his Alaska trips Muir lived and worked in the High Sierra, and as he studied its carved and scoured valleys, he became fairly obsessed with the action of glaciers in ages past. "The grandeur of these forces and their glorious results overpower me and inhabit my whole being. Waking or sleeping I have no rest. In dreams I read blurred sheets of glacial writing, or follow lines of cleavage, or struggle with the difficulties of some extraordinary rock-form."

After an outing in 1879 on what was later to be called Muir Glacier, he returned to Young in a state of ecstasy: "Man, man; you ought to have been with me. You'll never make up what you lost today. I've been wandering through a thousand rooms of God's crystal temple. I've been a thousand feet down in the crevasses, with matchless domes and sculptured figures and carved ice-work all about me. Solomon's marble and ivory palaces were nothing to it. Such purity, such color, such delicate beauty! I was tempted to stay there and feast my soul, and softly freeze, until I would become part of the glacier. What a great death that would be!"

In the nineteenth century, when geology was still a new and controversial science, glacier-study was an exciting, even urgent, pursuit. Scholars were just breaking away from the biblical interpretation of creation: that the world had been made in six days and that it was no more than about

5,000 or 6,000 years old. The idea that portions of the Northern Hemisphere had once been covered by glaciers, and that these glaciers — not the direct hand of God — had gouged valleys, polished granite, and shaped mountains, burst upon educated people everywhere with tremendous force. Such an idea demanded a different understanding of landscape, a different sense of time and scale, a new *Genesis*.

Muir was considered by many people of his age, the famed geologist John Tyndall among them, to have been the world's foremost expert on glaciers. In the Sierra he could study the effects of ancient glaciers; but in Alaska he could measure glacial movements, hear the grinding, and see with his own eyes the workings of "God's plow." Here he could "learn many new and wonderful facts about world-shaping"; here he could stand witness to the ongoing creation of the world.

Muir called his adventure with Stickeen "the most memorable of all my wild days." It was an experience that stayed with him throughout his life and shaped his thinking. Until his death at the age of seventy-six, Muir talked frequently of the little dog. He filled a large notebook with his thoughts about their day on the glacier, and he wrote many comments about it in the flyleaves of other books he owned. He told the story of Stickeen again and again. At parties or lectures it was said that waiters, porters, and servants would hide behind curtains or even under tables just to hear him tell the story.

For modern readers, *Stickeen* is pure tonic — bracing, refreshing, a charge of affirmation and joy. But for Muir that day on the glacier was also a revelation, presenting him with a piece of irreducible knowledge that was to change his very understanding of the world. Animal life was not highly regarded in the nineteenth century. Most biblical adherents held that animals lacked true intelligence, passion, and above all souls; animals had been placed on earth to fill people's needs. Advanced scientists of that day also diminished animals, holding them capable only of mechanical, instinctual responses to their environments. They too felt that humans alone had real understanding and passion, humans alone were capable of original thought.

Stickeen, however, revealed a different truth.

JOHN MUIR

It was as if the dog — driven to its utmost limits that day on the glacier — became momentarily transparent; and when Muir looked through to the essence of its being, what he saw in Stickeen was not very different from what he saw in himself. He and the dog were brothers, made of much the same stuff, differing from each other only in degree. "He enlarged my life," Muir wrote, "extended its boundaries . . . In all my wild walks seldom have I ever had a more definite and useful message to bring back. Stickeen was the herald of a new gospel." It was a gospel that Muir was to preach ardently the rest of his life, one that proclaimed the fundamental unity and sanctity of all living things.

Malcolm Margolin

Chronology of Muir's Life

1838 Born April 21 in Dunbar, Scotland; the third child and first son of a family of eight children.

1849 Family migrates to America and settles at Fountain Lake, Wisconsin, at that time the edge of wilderness.

1860 Gains local renown as an inventor of ingenious mechanical devices. Enters the University of Wisconsin at Madison.

1864 Makes a geological and botanical "tramp" around the Great Lakes and into Canada.

1865–66 Works in shops and factories, inventing and redesigning machinery, "busy almost to craziness . . . inventing machinery twenty-four hours a day."

1867 Undertakes "a thousand mile walk" from Kentucky through the war-ravaged south to Florida's Cedar Keyes, then on to Cuba.

1868 Arrives by boat in San Francisco, California, and immediately heads to the Sierra Nevada.

1869–72 Lives in Yosemite Valley, working first as a sheepherder in the high meadows, later as a sawyer in a Valley sawmill.

1873–76 Lives in Oakland and San Francisco. Begins writing articles about the geology and botany of the Sierra, frequently revisiting the mountains.

1877 Excursion to Utah in the spring. Then to Mount Shasta in late summer with botanists Joseph Hooker and Asa Gray. Muir returns to the San Francisco Bay area by canoeing down the Sacramento River.

1878 Employed by the U.S. Coast and Geodetic Survey to help survey parts of Nevada and Utah.

1879 First trip to Alaska. Discovers Glacier Bay.

1880 Marries Louie Wanda Strentzel. Returns to Alaska, and the adventure with Stickeen.

1881 Daughter, Anna Wanda, born. Muir joins an expedition to Alaska to search for the missing steamer, *Jeannette.*

1882 Begins actively managing the orchards of the Strentzel Ranch in Alhambra Valley, east of San Francisco Bay. Ranch business will absorb much of his energy for the next ten years.

1886 Second daughter, Helen, born. Travels with the artist, William Keith, to Vancouver, Puget Sound, and Mount Rainier.

1889 Becomes increasingly active in attempts to preserve the Sierra from overgrazing and logging, and to establish Yosemite Valley as a National Park.

1890 Another trip to Alaska.

1892 Leads in founding the Sierra Club, serving as president for the remainder of his life.

1893 Travels to the eastern United States and to Europe.

JOHN MUIR

1894 First major book, *Mountains of California*, published.

1896 Serves as an advisor to the commission that will review forest lands throughout the country and recommend to Congress the formation of forest reserves.

1897 "Stickeen" is first published as a story in *Century Magazine.*

1899 Joins John Burroughs, C. Hart Merriam, and other naturalists on a trip to Alaska sponsored by E. H. Harriman.

1903 Camps for three days in Yosemite Valley with Theodore Roosevelt. Two years later Roosevelt will establish Yosemite as a National Park. Travels to Europe, Siberia, Japan, China, India, and Australia.

1905 Wife dies. While visiting his daughter in the desert, he discovers the *Blue Forest* of petrified wood in Arizona.

1906 Instrumental in extending National Monument status to petrified forests.

1908 President Roosevelt sets aside a portion of the Grand Canyon as a National Monument, partly on Muir's recommendation. Muir becomes heavily involved in the attempt to save Hetch Hetchy Valley from flooding by a reservoir.

1909 *Stickeen* is first published in book form.

1911 Travels to South America and discovers groves of "monkey puzzle" trees in the Andes. Publication of *My First Summer in the Sierra*.

1912 Travels through Africa. Publication of *The Yosemite*.

1913 The Hetch Hetchy battle is lost. Publication of *Story of my Boyhood and Youth*.

1914 On Christmas Eve, John Muir dies. Manuscript pages of *Travels in Alaska* are scattered about his bed. Toward the end of his life he wrote on a scrap of paper: "Death is a kind of nurse saying, 'Come, children, to bed and get up in the morning,' — a gracious Mother calling her children home."